AF413745

Charlotte Valentina Taussig & Doris Taussig

HappyTottii finds love

Join HappyTottii on a Heartwarming Journey!

Meet HappyTottii, a little ladybug with a big heart who feels out of place in its community. Feeling sad and lonely, HappyTottii sets off on an adventure to find where it truly belongs. Along the way, our brave ladybug discovers the beauty of nature and learns the powerful lesson that love and acceptance are everywhere. Filled with exciting escapades and new friends, delightful story shows that sometimes, the greatest journey is the one that brings you back home. Perfect for bedtime reading, HappyTottii's tale will enchant young readers and reassure them that they are always loved.

On a morning like any other, little Tottii sat alone in a corner while the other ladybugs played together, their giggles filling the air with happiness. Tottii felt unloved and unnoticed. Despite wanting to approach the others and join their play, it lacked the courage to do so.

Tottii's biggest dream was to be part of the group, but it constantly felt rejected, repeating to itself: "Nobody loves me!", "Nobody wants to go explore with me!"

2

Even when picked up by its parents, Tottii
walked with a bent back and drooping head,
trudging home disappointed.

3

Arriving at the house, Tottii went to straight its room and felt a deep sense not to belong anywhere. Nobody recognized the beauty and talent. Asking itself: "Why is it so hard to be part of a group?"

Sad and full of sorrow, Tottii decided to run away.
It fled deep into the forest behind the house, which
was bursting with spring blossoms.
Flowers were blooming and the stream
flowed vigorousley, full of water from recent
rainy days. However, Tottii remained oblivious of the
surrounding beauty; all it wanted
to escape from everything and everyone.

5

Tottii ran and ran until it was almost out of breath.

6

When Tottii's legs could barely carry it further,
it stumbled apon a tree, sat down underneath
and fell asleep out of exhaustion.

7

All of a sudden a bright light danced around
Tottii and whispered:
"Open your eyes and you will see:
everything loves you."

8

Before the light vanished,
it left a glimmering spark in Tottii's eyes and spoke:
"The sparkle in your eyes shall always remind you
that love lives within yourself!"

9

Tottii woke up, stretched its wings, rubbed
its eyes, and opened them ... but did not see anything
special. Inspecting the flower left in front,
Tottii felt disappointed and did not understand what
the light had wanted to convey.

10

"I love you!", the flower suddenly said. Tottii was stunned and looked closer. In that very moment the flower opened up. Leaf after leaf, the flower began to unfold its beauty, revealing colours lovelier than Tottii had ever seen.

11

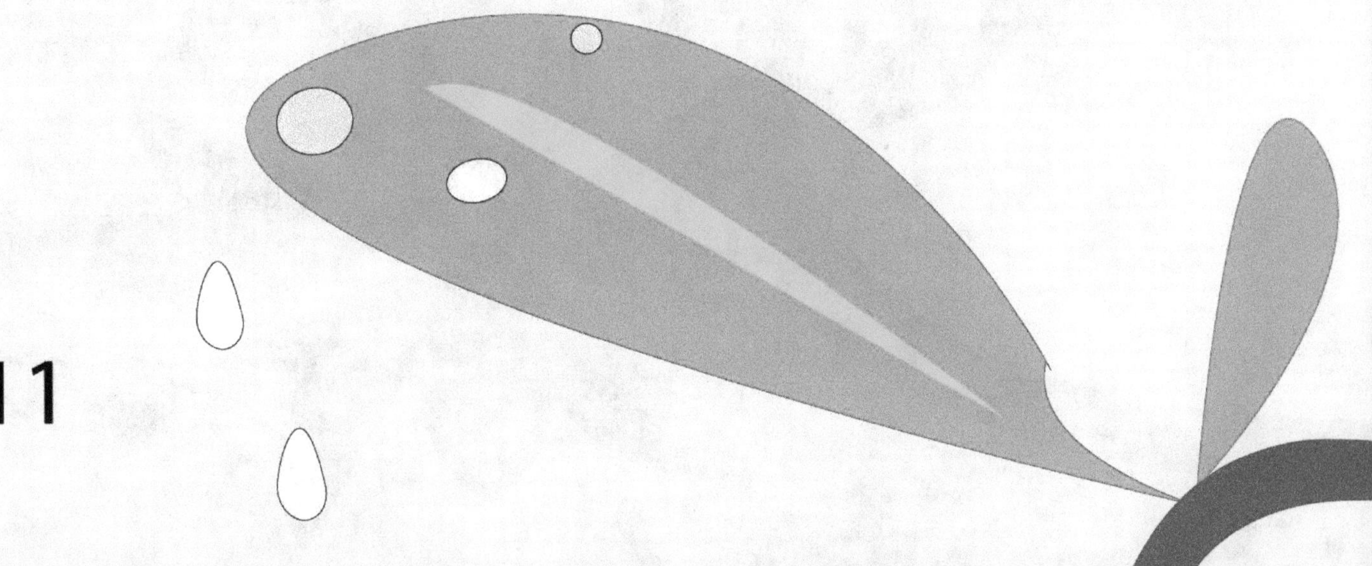

12

Tottii opened its eyes even wider and started to look around.
A wonderful tree stood tall with pride and confidence, its
branches invitingly open. Imitating the same confidence,
Tottii planted itself in front of the tree with back straight
and head held high.

"I love you", the tree said. All its leafs glowed with the freshest greens, rustling a song of love for Tottii.

14

Intrigued by the song, Tottii noticed the sound of the wind blowing through the leafs. The wind blew fiercely, hugging Tottii while whistling: "I love you." And so Tottii's last remaining doubts were blown away.

15

The concert continued, and Tottii heard
the brook murmuring: "I love you",
refreshing Tottii's outlook on life.

16

In a sudden sense of well-being, Tottii closed its eyes and
immediately felt the warming beams of the sun which seemed to say:
„I love you"

17

Tottii listened closer and noticed the tweeting
of singing birds completing the melody.
They, too were chirping: "We love you!"

18

Wherever Tottii looked and whatever it listened to,
it couldn't help but admire the beauty of uniqueness.
Everything loved Tottii! Gratitude and happiness
flowed through every vein and cell of Tottii's body.

19

Suddenly, Tottii remembered the love and affection
from its family and realized that they were surely missing it already.
After all, Tottii had been out for a long time.

21   Moving on its way, Tottii quickly became anxious to share
the discovery its family straight away.
Full of happiness and with a smile on its face, Tottii ran out of the forest.
On the way Tottii found an empty bottle and immediately threw it
into a trash can with happiness,
feeling satisfaction having done something for the environment.

When Tottii arrived home, the family was crying,
but the tears of sorrow soon turned into tears of love and happiness.
Tottii hugged each of them, and without words,
everyone felt how happy they were to be reunited again.

22

Tottii went to its room and looked in the mirror.
Full of confidence, it opened its wings and
admired their wonderful, mesmerizing colour.

23

24

Never before had Tottii noticed how utterly perfect its dots were, and
how lucky it was to have precisely seven of them.
Tottii's eyes lit up, and it finally saw the spark that the light had been talking about!
„I love you!" it giggled cheerfully to the reflection in the mirror.

25 „I love myself", Tottii now realized from the heart,
and the spark in its eyes grew even bigger and brighter.

26

After all these exciting adventures, Tottii felt tired.
It decided to lie down to ensure it would be happy,
refreshed, and glowing when it woke up by the next morning.

Like every day, the other ladybugs of Tottii's age were playing with each other, full of joy and excitement, and without paying no attention to Tottii. However this time, Tottii strolled straight over to them - upright and confident like the tree it had met the other day - and in a happy mood.

27

Tottii noticed that the other ladybugs were working on a puzzle and decided to find
the missing piece. „I got it!", Tottii shouted out and put the piece into its place.
Together they were able to complete the puzzle,
and everyone was grateful for Tottii's help.

28

It was the first time the others truly saw Tottii, and only now did they noticed
the spark in its eyes. They recognized its internal and external beauty and
the love Tottii carried inside. Tottii had become part of the group, and
they realized that they all belonged together.
From that day on, they called Tottii
"HappyTottii" because of the joy and love it spread.

Now HappyTottii understood what the light had wanted to tell it:
Only those who realize that love lies within
are able to see love everywhere.

30

HappyTottii ®

focused on love,
happiness,
nature,
envirionment

HappyTottii is not only art; it is a mission.
It represents something very new in the art world,
aiming to educate people globally in a gentle and
engaging manner about sustainable interactions with nature.
It highlights the importance of being mindful and
responsible with our actions concerning waste.
„HappyTottii finds love" is the introduction in HappyTottii's world.

Please note that, due to our policy,
we do not accept returns.
This decision aligns with HappyTottii's mission
to reduce waste and promote sustainability
on our planet.
Instead, we encourage you to consider
donating your items to schools,
individuals in need, or charitable organizations
that would greatly appreciate your generosity.
Thank you for your understanding and support.